IN EVERY WHISPER OF LOSS
LIES A THREAD,
WEAVING US INTO THE
INTRICATE DANCE OF CONNECTION

M.C.Bell.

ISBN: 979-8-9902001-5-9

Printed in USA
First Edition
For permission requests, write to the publisher at the address below:
The Grief Warrior®
Visit the author's website at www.michelecynthia.com

In the wake of losing my niece, an integral part of our family business and my daily life, I was lost in survivor's guilt and emotional turmoil. At 74, my successful business career had not prepared me for the depth of this loss. The accident left me navigating grief and a whirlwind of unresolved feelings, including intense rage and sadness.

Then, I encountered Michele. She ushered me into a space of grace and dignity, revealing a path of connection I hadn't known was possible. Guiding me through techniques to combat depression, reduce stress, and fully embrace the present, she made prayer, meditation, and conscious breathing part of my daily practice. Her 30-day challenges and the holistic support she offered, spanning from personal loss to business insights, catalyzed a transformative journey.

Michele led me to a profound state of gratitude. Encouraging me to write letters and share my innermost thoughts in a safe, authentic environment fostered a healing I hadn't imagined. She rekindled joy in my life, showing me that profound transformation is attainable at any age. Her expertise and genuine presence revitalized me, giving me back to myself healthier and more vibrant.

Through Michele, I discovered the power of connection, skillfully threading my story into the broader mosaic of life and connection.

– MICHAEL W. HUMPHREY

Foundation of

EMBRACE

Prelude to Stage Six

This foundational section provides a comprehensive overview of *The 7 Stages of Grief*, setting the stage for the deep dive into **CONNECT** that follows. While it serves as an introduction, it is designed to be revisited, offering insight and context as you navigate through each stage of your journey.

The EMBRACE Journey
Transform Grief and
Discover Inner *Strength*

Welcome, Warriors, to the extraordinary dimension of the 7 Stages of Grief Workbook Journal. I will guide you through a miraculous and empowering passage, unveiling the hidden treasures amidst the labyrinth of trauma and loss.

This course was born from my authentic desire to *heal it forward* in the grief community, ignited by theta meditation and a deep desire to manifest growth and healing through my writings. Drawing upon my intuitive theta-visions, I have created the EMBRACE framework — a radiant constellation of seven stages illuminating our transformative expedition in the wake of adversity.

In contrast to conventional approaches that merely skim the surface of emotions within the limited confines of the five stages of grief, I sensed the dire need for a holistic and transformative tapestry. The 7 stages of grief, meticulously crafted through my Healing it Forward modalities used in my 1:1 sacred retreats, transcend the ephemeral realm of emotions, ushering us into a realm where storytelling, the sacred utterance of our beloved's name, and the cultivation of gratitude mingle, guiding us through each challenging obstacle that graces our path.

Within this cherished community of kindred souls, we will unite, bound by a shared mission to collaborate, share our truth, and breathe life into one another's spirits—a sacred alchemy that fosters a radiant cascade of healing and metamorphosis. The modalities unveiled in the EMBRACE workbook journal's resplendent pages revolutionized how we navigate our sacred inner landscape, transforming the lives of those who have an unwavering longing to embrace the transformative work ahead.

As an extraordinary boon, I invite you to journey beside me as a Certified Grief Wellness Warrior, armed with the profound and purposeful modalities needed to extend a gentle hand to those ensnared in the clutches of their grief. By immersing yourself in these transformative practices and obtaining certification, you shall illuminate the path for others in their darkest moments, serving as a beacon of light and hope amidst the unfathomable abyss.

With deepest gratitude and genuine admiration, I extend my heartfelt appreciation to you for summoning the courage to embark upon the sacred journey of the EMBRACE workbook journal course. I assure you, Warriors, that this decision shall cascade with blessings and profoundly resonate. Together, let us traverse the infinite depths of grief, unlocking the wellspring of our inner fortitude and embarking upon a journey that transcends healing alone—a voyage brimming with purpose, renewal, and the willful power of the human spirit.

Prepare yourself for the transformational power of the 7 Stages of Grief Workbook Journal.

Let our extraordinary odyssey begin.

The Grief Warrior

Table of Contents

FOREWARD

My name is Cristal Sampson, and I work in mental health and psychiatry as a nurse practitioner in the UK, Connecticut, and New York, specializing in traumatic stress and mood disorders. I am also a young woman who experienced an early-term spontaneous miscarriage that burned a hole in depths I had previously not known existed. The revelation of this new depth of unconditional love, coupled with my baby's teeny heart stopping, left me hollow.

Even in my subsequent pregnancy the following year, I still felt empty of the unfulfillable desire for the baby back that I had lost in this life. The emptiness was filled with sadness, anxiety, and disappointment from troubled family dynamics – *a family unaware of my loss and grief.*

Someone with my expertise is never immune to the heartaches of the human experience, such as the loss of love and life. I recognized the potential to become an emotionally absent mother to my unborn baby, a fate that seemed all but certain at the time – and the thought terrified me. I am grateful to have understood that both my baby and I deserved the opportunity to heal. In my research, I discovered Michele, The Grief Warrior®.

As a health professional and a mental health specialist, I am particularly discerning about the services I opt for and the providers I choose. During this chapter of my life and given the circumstances, I did not pursue "traditional" mental health counseling. At that moment, confronting the challenges presented by contemporary therapy seemed beyond my capacity. I perceived the potential for a more conventional approach to be beneficial later in my healing journey.

What Michele provided touched the very core, breadth, and depth of my pain, reaching deep into the spiritual, mental, emotional, and energetic aspects of my being, body, and environment through a one-on-one retreat. I have not encountered anything like it since. Therefore, I am deeply moved that you are here, exploring the 7 Stages of Grief. Your journey with Michele's intentional energy, as conveyed through her books, and her custom human design modalities coupled with her healing energy, will extensively shift your essence and transform you.

FOREWARD

The 'EMBRACE: The 7 Stages of Grief' workbook series is designed to support every individual navigating grief—those who feel unprepared and overwhelmed by the complexities of losing a loved one. This series speaks to the heart of those oscillating between the anticipation of loss and the necessity of maintaining 'normalcy,' amidst the swirl of anger, resentment, and sorrow. It is a compassionate companion for every silent sufferer, for those caught in the emotional storm of impending loss, and for caregivers in dire need of nurturing themselves.

What distinguishes Michele's 'The 7 Stages of Grief' series most is the infusion of practical hope within its pages—a hope that is both tangible and deeply rooted in the natural spaces where resilience and healing begin. Michele brings a deep understanding and mastery in guiding others through the vast resources available for grief support, offering pathways that are both practical and easily navigable. Her insight into the caregiver journey, as a single mother is profoundly intimate, shaped by her own experience of lovingly supporting her teenage son, through his transition, enveloped in a cocoon of love. This unique perspective enriches her approach, making her guidance not only informed but deeply empathetic to the nuanced experiences of grief.

My work with Michele has caused a seismic shift in my perspective and has improved my relationships with myself, my family, and the people who meet me. I am moved with infinite gratitude at the positive and priceless impact my work with Michele has had on my experience of motherhood and the beautiful relationship my daughter and I get to have. Now, I enjoy expanding my connection as she has become a selfless friend and true mentor.

I encourage you to allow this book to transform you positively. Let it be a daily source of support and comfort, especially in moments of need. Remember, everything Michele has undertaken since Nicky's return to the Source has been a heartfelt ode to him and a homage to the enduring legacy of love and purpose he entrusted to her. Michele's ultimate wish is for you to discover your purpose and allow it to drive you forward through the cherished journey of your life.

Cristal Sampoon

FROM MY HEART
to yours...

Alignment in the face of loss is the only option. When we open ourselves to the possibilities presented to us, we find this harmony: in the strength of our words, in the peace of our meditations, in the gift of our presence, in the renewal of our bodies, in the stirring of our spirits, in the depth of our relationships, and in the nourishment we give ourselves.

The path to recovery is a beautiful tapestry that offers the opportunity for personal development and the forging of inner fortitude. We will brave new territory together, learn new things, and grow as people. I will be your guide and source of solace throughout our journey together. Get ready to reclaim your life with renewed confidence as you learn to swiftly navigate life's complications and unleash your remarkable inner potential.

There is nothing scary or complicated about this course since I will be there to guide you through every one of the steps. Let's take off on a journey into the unknown, where the payoff to SELF could be infinite.

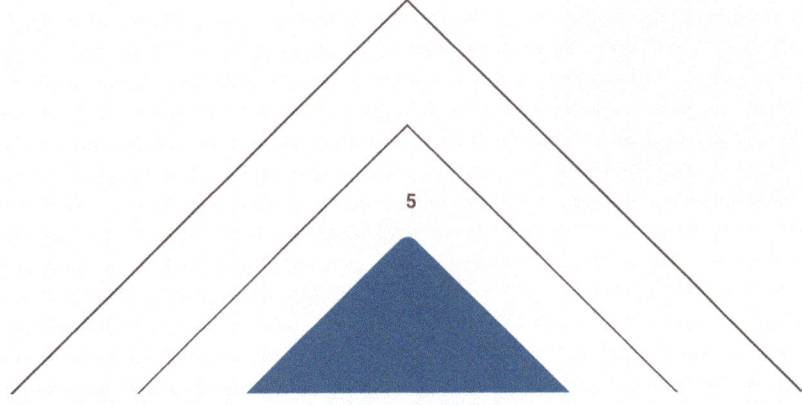

PROLONGED GRIEF DISORDER
Unveiled
as total B.S

Shattering the Illusion: Liberating Ourselves from the Constraints of the "5 Stages of Grief"

Adhering to established norms is a delusion, a fallacy we must quickly let go of when dealing with extended grief disorder. The "5 Stages of Bereavement" model developed by psychologists has been widely disseminated for too long, permeating every aspect of grief counseling and education.

Unfortunately, the constant push to conform to a set and narrow path of grieving has led me and countless other seekers within the grief community to feel disillusioned.

I beg you to disregard this erroneous advice immediately. The core meaning of our name, "EMBRACE," contains the whole truth. The concept of "Prolonged Grief Disorder" is 100% bogus.

The "5 Stages of Grief" concept originated from an unsupported theory meant to characterize the reaction of people who had been given fatal diagnoses rather than those who were navigating the maze of loss and sorrow. Here we have two utterly dissimilar yet actual experiences, each of which calls for special attention and comprehension.

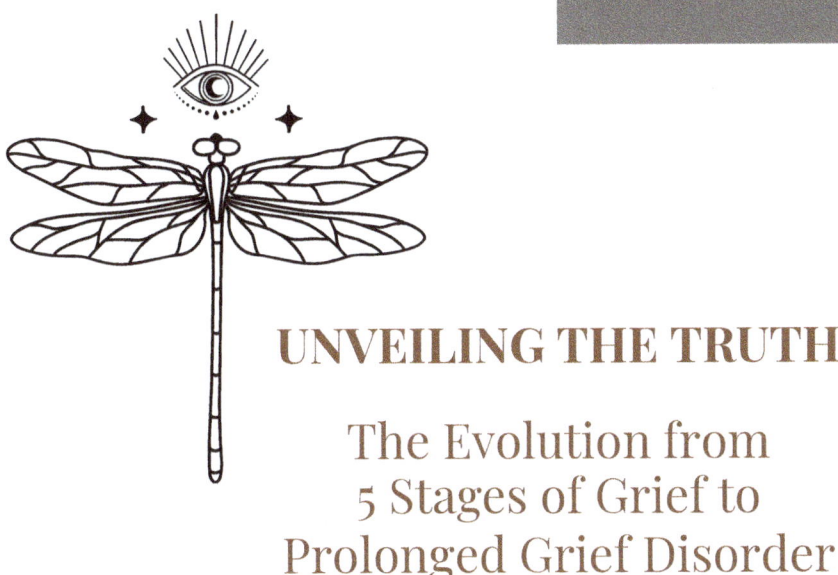

UNVEILING THE TRUTH

The Evolution from 5 Stages of Grief to Prolonged Grief Disorder

In March 2022, a new grief-related disorder was officially adopted into mainstream mental health diagnosis nomenclature. Seeing how the clinical world has further shamed the sacred grieving world is disheartening. DSM-5's trauma and stress-related category have a new label: Prolonged Grief Disorder, created deliberately to define what grief should and should not look like.

But first, let's take a moment to think. What exactly is this thing called "Prolonged Grief Disorder"? Claiming a year for adults and a paltry six months for children is an arrogant attempt to restrict the complex fabric of grief inside the confines of time. According to the American Psychological Association, persons who carry this label are assumed to exhibit the following symptoms even after the diagnostic window has closed:

- The crushing weight of grief pressed down on every aspect of their being.
- An unending fixation on sorrow as memories of the lost reverberate ceaselessly.
- A mental panorama obscured by agony or the unsettling absence of feeling.
- They engage in a delicate dance of denial and avoidance as they try to face their loved one's death.
- Dissonance and disconnection can develop when one feels different from the social norm.
- Every breath is filled with the haunting repercussions of despair and isolation.

We stand at the intersection of societal, cultural, and religious expectations, where the mere fulfillment of established criteria has become pivotal in making a prognosis. Understandably, when engulfed by the darkness of losing a loved one, such clinical classifications may not bring the peace and comprehension one wants.

To promote genuine healing, we need to permit ourselves to explore our inner emotional landscape freely.

Let us stand up as one in our resolve to overcome this stereotype's obstacles. Let us regain our freedom from societal norms to grieve and heal as we see fit.

We will overcome obstacles as a group and EMBRACE the journey of getting to the heart of our pain and reclaiming our ways forward in healing.

WHY PROLONGED GRIEF DISORDER
is Facing So Much Criticism

01

There is no moral compass in the arena of mourning.

Grief isn't reducible to a single feeling but incorporates many of them. It weaves a complex and ever-changing mosaic of emotions, including sadness, rage, anguish, loneliness, reverence, connection, and perplexity.

It's a shared adventure that everyone does on their terms.

Grief is complex and multifaceted: No two souls mourn alike, for no two losses are identical. Attempts to confine the grieving process within cookie-cutter stages, rigid criteria, and prescribed timelines propagate the fallacy of a right or wrong way to grieve.

02

Grief, in its essence, is a natural phenomenon—

A sacred dance that unfolds within the depths of our being. It is a deeply personal and profound experience, far from being a pathological problem to be solved.

A child's heart carries the imprint of a parent's absence for months or years. Similarly, a parent's longing for a child, partner, or loved one transcends all notions of time. The ache, the longing, lives in the very essence of our human nature.

03

Grief is an enigmatic path; Grief isn't linear.—

If we were to create a line graph of our grief journeys, it would be surprising for scientists to discover no discernible pattern.

Within the ebb and flow of our grief, we encounter good and bad days interwoven in a twisted dance.

Embracing this is how we move with our grief. Labeling and attempting to confine it only breeds resistance. Progress lies *not* in imposing a specific timeline but in surrendering to the ever-changing flow of our grief and learning to move on with acceptance and dignity.

04

Grief isn't inherently harmful.

Grief is evidence of love lost.

It serves as a poignant symbol of our love, our desire to cherish and remember those individuals and relationships that hold deep significance in our lives.

It's instinctively human: both beautiful and painful. By labeling grief as a problem in this sacred space, By labeling grief as a problem to solve, we carry it. By leaning into our pain, we *move with* it.

05

Grief looms of isolation. Support becomes our lifeline.

Grief defies measurement, transcending the confines of milestones as the 5 Stages of Grief imply. It is an ever-evolving journey, an ongoing experience. Pathologizing and diagnosing grief makes it feel abnormal. In reality, it represents so much of the human experience.

Diagnoses can empower us by illuminating how our minds or bodies function differently and offering solutions. However, diagnosing grief only deepens the shame, loneliness, and isolation. No one should feel wrong for grieving beyond a specific date.

We need grief support, not grief diagnosis. By creating space for its expression, allowing its capacity to unfold without restraint.

Unlock the Profound Power of Healing with EMBRACE
The 7 Stages of Grief Alignment

Are you prepared to immerse yourself on a journey of healing and self-discovery?

Step into a sphere of authenticity, truth, and love as you immerse yourself in the unparalleled wisdom and guidance offered in the transformative EMBRACE course. This course goes beyond the ordinary, offering a depth of healing that will leave an indelible impact.

What sets EMBRACE apart? It emerges from the heart of an expert grief practitioner, infused with the spirit of authenticity and infused by a genuine desire to empower and support individuals on their unique healing journeys.

EMBRACE offers a transformative approach that transcends traditional teachings.

Through this meticulously crafted course, you will unlock the tools and techniques to navigate the depths of grief, embracing healing and growth. The 7 Stages of Grief Alignment workbook becomes your trusted companion, providing compassionate guidance through each stage. It empowers you to honor your journey, embrace your emotions, and pave the way for a purposeful shift.

However, EMBRACE's path forward still needs to be completed. Those interested in learning more and becoming certified "Healing it Forward" practitioners will find that this course provides a beautiful opportunity to do just that. As a trained professional, you will be honored to assist others on their journey to wholeness and personal development.

The EMBRACE program is an astonishing journey of self-discovery and empowerment, not simply another healing class. It encourages you to look within, where you'll find the key to your inner wisdom and the key to your recovery. Along the journey, you'll be surrounded and transformed by a community of like-minded spirits who share your unyielding dedication to growth and give support and encouragement.

Are you prepared to take your life's most incredible life-changing healing journey? Join us on this life-altering adventure, where our north stars are sincerity, honesty, and love. Learn the true meaning of pivoting with intent through your experience with EMBRACE. Your healing journey awaits, and we are here to walk alongside you every step of the way.

Are You Ready?

ALL RIGHT, GRIEF WARRIORS:

We're breaking up with the 5 Stages of Grief

Meet your new boo,
the 7 Stages of Grief Alignment!

The 7 Stages of Grief Alignment knows no order. They are not
steps but continual pillars, symbols, and actions to make
space for grief in your growth.

*Words hold immense power, and we choose to
transform our grief rather than diagnose it.*

The Grief Warrior

EMBRACE

THE 7 STAGES OF GRIEF ALIGNMENT

01

EXPRESS
Let your emotions guide you and experience the joy and fulfillment of expressing your true self through journaling and artistic exploration.

02

MEDITATE
Embrace the power of sitting with your grief, opening your heart, and leaning into the serenity of the present moment, creating space for healing and growth.

03

BE PRESENT
Pause. Observe and relinquish the need for constant busyness, and tune into the depths of your feelings. Embrace the beauty, opportunity, and purpose in this moment.

04

REJUVENATE
Reignite your zest for life, nourish your soul, and elevate your vibrations through the transformative power of self-care. Rediscover what it means to feel truly alive.

05

AWAKEN
Awaken the part of you that's been hiding. Reclaiming lost joy, energy, and vibrance. Rediscover the essence of your true self, waiting to be revealed.

06

CONNECT
Grief can separate us from true ourselves, making us feel like trapped observers of our lives. Reconnect physically, mentally, and spiritually to find your center and regain a sense of control and profound connection.

07

EAT HEALTHY
Nourish your body with the fuel it craves for strength and vitality. Embrace the sensory delight of flavors, textures, and intuitive connection as your body receives each healthy bite.

What 'stage' speaks to you?

IF YOU'RE READY TO TURN YOUR PAIN INTO FUEL...

Your past can lead you to your purpose.

Your pain can become your fuel to embody and fulfill that purpose. It's time to heal the resilient spirit within you, the one who has overcome more than imagined possible.

Unclench your jaw. Let out a sigh of relief - and stop running. We can't change our pasts. e may not alter our pasts, but we can find peace in our history and shape our futures by nurturing our souls in the present moment.

Each of us possesses a unique narrative shaped by our experiences. While we may not always have control over the plot, we have the power to choose the underlying theme. Let us craft our stories around the essence of healing rather than being defined by pain.

Rise as a warrior, not just a survivor. I am here to guide you because I believe in your strength.

It's time to take hold of the reins and chart a path toward healing, love, and inner strength.

i believe in you.

Grab a pen, and we'll embark on your new journey together.

> *Your past paves the path to purpose.*

PIVOT *with* PURPOSE

My vocation is a sacred calling, where every word, line, and page is carefully crafted with intention and purpose. My vocation extends far beyond the conventional realms. It transcends the boundaries of traditional academia and ventures into the realm of energy and transcendence.

Having traversed the depths of deep trauma and loss, I intimately understand the weight of grief and despair. Yet, I alchemize that suffering into meaning through the art of writing, creating, and teaching. I am fueled by authentic and intentional love in every breath of my life.

It is not a love born out of obligation but a love that empowers and inspires, beckoning others to rise above their fears and embrace the limitless possibilities that lie within them.

To me, this is the very essence of sacredness.

Let this inspire you that, no matter your challenges, you can *Pivot with Purpose* and manifest life in alignment with your highest energy. As your Grief Warrior® mentor, I will guide you on a sacred transformation journey.

The Grief Warrior

I HAD TWO CHOICES:

Retreat Or Renew

When my first-born son passed away, grief consumed me. I could have withdrawn from life, but a fire within me refused to give up. It was then that I realized grief is the expression of love. It's our mind and heart's way of grappling with loss. It requires embracing the unknown, for life itself is unpredictable, regardless of our beliefs.

In rediscovering the magic of life, I rekindled my commitment to live truly. The grief didn't vanish, but it became more manageable. I started noticing the small things that bring joy to life. Each day became an adventure filled with endless possibilities. With an open heart, I welcomed the uncertainties that came my way. While the aftermath of a loss can leave us feeling hopeless, the strength to persevere can lead to unexpected achievements. Withdrawing may seem tempting, but it only perpetuates a downward spiral. We can move forward and rediscover joy by renewing our commitment to purposeful living.

I crafted the 7 Stages of Grief Alignment to renew my commitment—a guide from eleven years of personal experience and introspection. My book, A Son's Gift, became a testament to living intentionally after unforeseen circumstances. This challenge navigates the unexpected tragedies that may befall us, particularly if we face intense grief for the first time. Each stage holds significance, and we must traverse them daily. It isn't always easy, but a life infused with meaning and purpose is worthwhile.

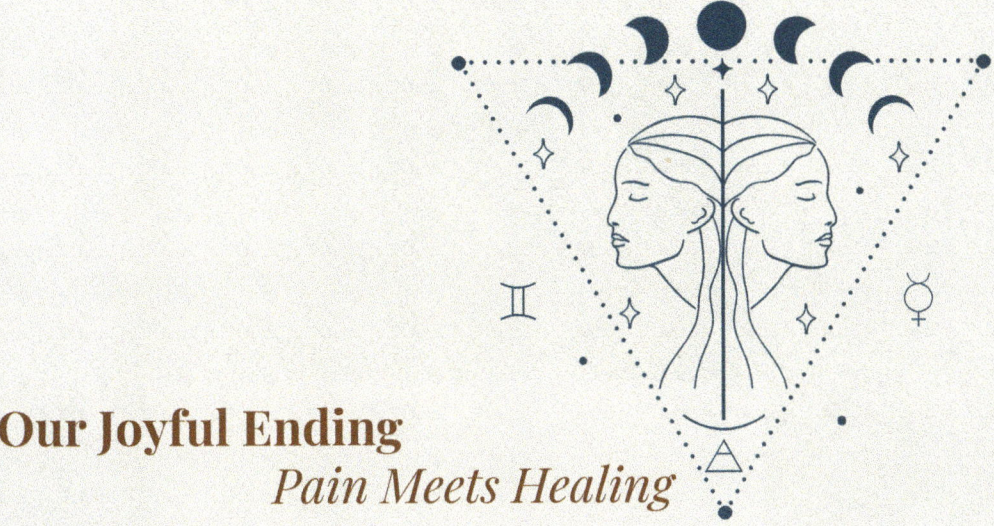

Our Joyful Ending
Pain Meets Healing

Once upon a time,

...in the whimsical land of Serenityville, a group of courageous warriors known as the Serene Seekers set forth on a remarkable quest—the Journey of Healing it Forward. Guided by the wise and enchanting fairy Seraphina, they discovered the secret power of acceptance. The goal was to align with the 7 Stages of Grief and release the mystical power inside.

The Serene Seekers set out on their journey full of bravery and love. As they wandered through enchanted forests and sparkling waterways, they experienced times of hardship. They didn't shy away since they knew the answer to their problems resided within themselves.

The Serene Seekers blazed a trail based on the ancient wisdom of the 7 Stages of Grief Alignment. Each phase—"Express," "Meditate," "Be Present," "Rejuvenate," "Awaken," "Connect," and "Eat Healthy"—held a vital piece of the puzzle to their recovery and development.

Under Seraphina's guidance, the Serene Seekers learned that pain was not their enemy but a teacher to be embraced. It became a part of their story, a testament to their courage and resilience. United in their journey, they supported one another, sharing stories and offering solace when needed. Their empathy and compassion wove a love web across Serenityville.

By embracing their pain, the Serene Seekers discovered the profound magic of healing it forward. They realized their healing could inspire and uplift others, spreading hope and resilience far and wide.

The Serene Seekers' journey through the 7 Stages of Grief Alignment showcased the power of acceptance and showed the world how beautiful it can be. Their travels exemplified the concept of "healing it forward," the idea that one person's kindness may positively impact others.

And so, the Serene Seekers continued their noble quest, fueled by determination and love. Together, they embarked on the Journey of Healing It Forward, embracing their pain, sharing their stories, and spreading seeds of healing throughout Serenityville and beyond.

This uplifting tale illustrates the power of facing our suffering and moving with "Healing it Forward."

HOW TO
Sit *with* Your Grief

ACKNOWLEDGE IT.

OWN IT.

EXPLORE IT.

THERE ARE 3 FUNDAMENTAL

STEPS TO EMBRACING YOUR GRIEF

FEEL *and* ACKNOWLEDGE IT

Feel - Dive into the Depths of Emotion In the first step. We will learn the art of feeling. Relax your body and mind by closing your eyes and taking a few slow, deep breaths. Don't oppose or judge the feelings you're experiencing.

Are you on the verge of purging, overwhelmed by a storm of pain, guilt, shame, betrayal, or envy?

In EMBRACE, you will understand the depth of your pain through emotional exploration. Embracing our feelings shows respect for the integrity of our experience and lays the foundation for healing.

To *acknowledge* is to embrace the power of acceptance with the courage to feel. It is easy to dismiss our grief, burying it beneath layers of denial or self-judgment. But this step teaches us to embrace our pain by acknowledging its presence. Let go of the urge to push your feelings aside or berate yourself for struggling. Instead, recognize that grief is a natural and valid experience. When you own your suffering, you allow yourself the time and perspective to determine what's causing it.

OWN YOUR FEELINGS
of Pain, Grieving, Loss

Understanding your feelings is the first step, but owning your pain is crucial. Grief is often associated with a side of ourselves that we prefer to ignore, so we dismiss it. However, pushing your emotions aside or criticizing yourself for struggling can worsen things. Instead, it's essential to accept your pain as a natural and valid experience and take responsibility for it.

By holding yourself accountable, you can create the space and understanding necessary to delve deeper into the issue and uncover its root cause. This process of self-exploration allows you to work with your pain rather than fighting against it, leading to gradual healing and release from its grasp. With time, you may find that your pain becomes a source of wisdom and inspiration, helping you cultivate self-compassion, acceptance, and strength.

So, don't dismiss your pain or judge yourself for feeling it. Embrace it as an opportunity for self-discovery and growth, and let it guide you on your journey.

ARE YOU LIVING A LIFE *of Denial?*

Denial is a tempting refuge, an escape from facing the truth that awaits us. But is it truly living?

Yet, in denying our true selves, we rob life of its vibrant colors. We become sleepwalkers, traversing existence without truly seeing or experiencing its wonders. Disconnected from our emotions, we numb ourselves to the essence of our being, avoiding the aspects of life we dare not confront.

Grief has a way of leaving us feeling empty, disconnected from the world. Faced with such turbulent emotions, it is crucial to remain present. Opening ourselves to the surrounding reality allows us to reestablish our connection to ourselves and the world surrounding us.

If denial has become your shield for too long, it is time to confront the truth. Though it may be a painful pilgrimage, evading your emotions and sidestepping the obstacles that impede your growth will only perpetuate your suffering. To live a life of integrity and authenticity, we must be brave enough to acknowledge our wounds and fears.

Embrace the journey, for it may come with its share of challenges. Remember, transformation is not an overnight process; it requires time and intense dedication. But as you courageously confront your pain, you will uncover hidden wells of strength within. Say goodbye to denial and welcome the truth of your existence. With each intentional step, you carve a path toward a life filled with authenticity and purpose.

The path ahead may be arduous, but you are not alone. I am here to offer my unwavering support, accompanying you through every stride of this transformative journey. Embrace your inner resilience and have faith in the healing process.

Trust yourself and step boldly into a life of authenticity and growth. You have the power to rewrite your story.

The Guiding Light of *Embrace*
Nurturing Those in Grief

Faced with another's grief, we often find ourselves at a loss for words. The profound pain and sorrow they bear can leave us powerless, uncertain of how to offer solace in their darkest hours. Yet, amidst the vastness of this challenge, there exists a flare of hope—a well-crafted grief book, EMBRACE.

In these pages, you'll find a companion journal that will bring comfort and understanding to those roaming the twisted path of sorrow.

While it is impossible to erase the pain, EMBRACE can soothe the aching heart and guide one's steps through the obstacles of grief.

The sentimental narratives make the emotions' kaleidoscope more explicit and the burden of grief more tolerable. As a treasured tool in your grief bag, the 7 Stages of Grief Alignment provides a roadmap for the griever and their companions, fostering awareness and healing.

Yet, it is crucial to remember that when supporting someone living in grief, the gift of your presence and enduring willingness to listen outweighs any words of wisdom or reassurance.

With its intricate nuances, grief often leaves those who mourn feeling isolated and misunderstood. EMBRACE is a heartfelt promise that assures you that you are not alone in your journey.

EMBRACE will offer hope and encouragement, reminding readers they are not alone in their sorrow. Consider giving them a copy to support a friend or loved one during grief.

If you want to support a friend or loved one during grief, consider giving them a copy of EMBRACE! You want the support of your loved ones, and the same goes for them needing you. As with any journey in life, the journey of grief as a team, we got this!

The Healing Dance of Grief
Nurturing the Spirit *within*

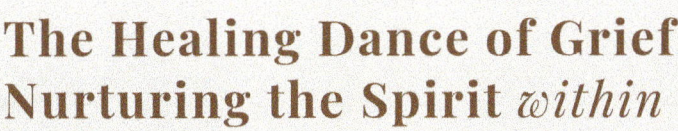

When someone close to us dies tragically, we are engulfed by an overwhelming sense of loss, accompanied by a symphony of painful emotions. We journey through this dimension of grief, uniquely navigating its twists and turns. Some shed tears like raindrops from a stormy sky, others ignite with fiery anger, while some retreat into the solitude of their inner world. These reactions, these expressions of grief, are the rivers that flow from the depths of our souls. We must honor them, for within these expressions lie the seeds of self-awareness and the catalysts for healing.

It's simple to feel disoriented and overwhelmed in today's fast-paced, ever-evolving society. The grieving process is a multifaceted test; we all long for the loving company of a compassionate that requires us to seek comfort from those who can relate. As a holistic practitioner, I stand ready with the tools and resources to accompany you on this sacred pilgrimage. Drawing upon my extensive experience, I offer a sanctuary where your voice can be heard, your story shared, and your healing ignited.

Discerning the way forward is exhausting in life's chaotic orchestra, where confusion and uncertainty reign. The weight of emotional pain may tempt us to forge ahead, mindlessly seeking an escape from the obstacles that hinder our progress. Yet, dear soul, a profound wellspring of resilience and strength lies within you. Developing spiritual growth can lead to a limitless abundance of peace and stability. Nurturing your connection with a higher power or the wisdom within you can help you navigate life's most brutal storms with grace and serenity. As you enter this sacred journey of spiritual expansion, you will uncover newfound capacities to navigate life's turbulent seas, supporting your passage and extending a loving hand to those who traverse similar paths.

The road may appear dimly lit as you tread its winding path. Yet, within you resides a radiance of faith, highlighting the darkness for those who desire comfort in your presence. Even when grief looms, keep hope alive in the sanctuary of your heart. I encourage optimism even in the darkness. Envision a shining star, your inner strength shining its light into the deepest crevices of despair. As you gaze upon the darkness, challenge fear and vulnerability to manifest and transform into a conduit for healing. By embracing the full spectrum of your being, shadows, and all, you control the destiny of self-empowerment. Even in the trenches of darkness, your intense light inspires and uplifts those who witness your strength and courage.

Remember that you are never alone in the sacred dance of grief, where each step is steeped with the essence of unconditional love. Reach out, Warrior, to those who can guide and support you on this transformative pilgrimage. Together, you will honor the pain, nurture your spirit, and spin a tapestry of healing that extends far beyond the realms of grief. Let the rhythm of your heart guide you, as it holds within it the tune of perseverance, the harmony of optimism, and the assurance of rejuvenation.

Shadows become tools that help shape
Who You Are...

The Symphony of *Empathy* Navigating Responses to *Grief*

Why do some people run when I embrace my sadness?

Have you ever felt alone in your sadness because others choose to ignore or withdraw from you?

It's disheartening to question whether you deserve support or understanding. It can be challenging for those not accustomed to dealing with intense emotions like grief to face their feelings. Fear, unfamiliarity, and a lack of knowledge about responding supportively could all contribute to their feelings.

It can feel like others are trying to hide from the truth of your experience and being when they avoid hearing about your sorrowful tale. It might make you feel invisible, alone, and desperate for approval. An essential part of the grieving process is vulnerability, which searches for comfort in human connection and comprehension.

However, it is essential to note that only some can face and hold space for strong emotions, especially if they have not experienced something comparable. Their insecurity stems from a need for more ease with showing emotion. It's important not to take their reaction personally; instead, give yourself time and space to work through your feelings.

Be gentle with yourself and embrace the understanding that not everyone will comprehend or offer enduring support on this path. With time, you'll meet people who can hold the sacred space for your grief, opening doors to vital life lessons and opportunities for new relationships.

There can be many reasons why people don't respond to your melancholy expressions. Some people may struggle with displays of intense emotion, while others may feel ill-equipped to respond to someone who is deeply sorrowful. In certain instances, people may even fear that witnessing your sadness will awaken their dormant pain. It is essential to acknowledge that each person uniquely navigates grief, and adverse reactions to your sorrow do not show a lack of care or concern. Give them breathing room to deal with their feelings; they may discover the strength to help you.

As you continue your grief journey, remember that your emotions are valid and that your need for support is real. Seek solace in those who can hold space for your grief, and let go of the notion that everyone will understand. The dance of empathy requires patience and calls for self-compassion. If you care for yourself during this process, you show others how accepting melancholy can strengthen the spirit.

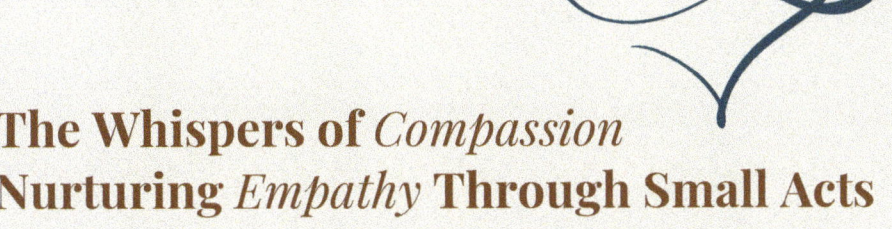

The Whispers of *Compassion* Nurturing *Empathy* Through Small Acts

Empathy's complex webs of connection strengthen relationships during the grieving process. A kind touch, reassuring words, and a listening ear can go a long way toward alleviating emotional pain. During sadness, expressions of sympathy transform into a beautiful melody of support, kindness, and concern.

Even the tiniest gestures can convey the magnitude of affection and concern in moments of quiet reflection. Sincerity and love injected into the most straightforward actions can illuminate the darkest places. These seemingly insignificant acts go beyond words to bring solace to the soul. By doing these nice things for them, we can let them know they have our undying support and are not alone.

Sometimes, the answer lies not in words but in the silent embrace of companionship. To stand beside someone in their darkest hours to honor their wishes can transcend an act of compassion. You become a sanctuary of support for their wounded soul. Becoming a lifeline amidst the chaos by offering practical help, running errands, and preparing nourishing meals demonstrates that our warmth extends beyond mere words to sacred stillness.

They provide a sympathetic ear that accepts their suffering without judgment or making demands. We become instruments of compassion and wisdom, holding the door open for their recovery.

When words fail, being there and knowing how grateful we are can help comfort a broken spirit. Therefore, let us recognize the significance of greeting cards, reassuring embraces, and quiet moments of reflection. Aim to personify empathy, compassion, and concern. We become the vessels through which comfort is delivered, mending the broken parts of a mourning person's spirit in those quiet times.

You can use the following phrases:

My heart goes out to you; I'm sorry this is happening to you.
"What is your loved one's name?"
"What do you say we get some lunch together? Please tell me more about (insert name of cherished one here)."

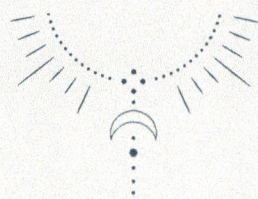

The Unseen Language of Sorrow
Embracing *Understanding* and *Letting Go*

It's frustrating when those close to you don't understand how much your loss means to you. Some wonder if avoiding those who can't share our sorrow is right. But let's PAUSE to think about this:

No matter how well you articulate your pain, not everyone can comprehend complex emotions. Despite our efforts to articulate our pain, some may struggle to grasp its true essence. In these situations, letting go of our dependence on their comprehension is not a sign of a lack of strength or inability. Our efforts to help them understand the inexplicable would be well-spent.

Don't you think it's wonderful to imagine a world where empathy is cultivated and understanding becomes a part of our collective etiquette? While that ideal may be far off, we can take comfort in the company of those who share our values and offer proper understanding and support. Seek comfort in knowing you are not alone on your grief journey. By doing so, we create space for our healing, allowing our sorrow to unfold in its way, guided by our resilience and the support of those who truly understand.

01 Let us find comfort in the arms of those who truly understand and share our pain on this developing path of sorrow. Even if others can't understand our pain, it's reassuring that some would listen with empathy and provide a safe place to heal.

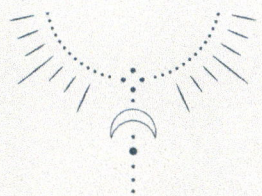

02

In the depths of sorrow, we are faced with a "griefosophical" lesson:

We are the chosen ones entrusted with the sacred duty of carrying the unseen language of sorrow. It is not a burden to bear but a calling that sets us apart from others. Our connection with our departed loved one runs deep, transcending the comprehension of others. The love we shared with them was unique, profound, and intimate, coloring our grief in hues that may mystify those who did not experience the same depth of connection.

Rather than harboring resentment or seeking understanding from those who cannot offer it, we can shift our perspective. It helps to think of ourselves as spiritual vessels that have solemnly promised to bear the burden of our grief. To mourn together is to witness the strength of love and reveal the depth of our connection.

By letting go of the expectation that everyone will understand our grief, we unlock a sense of communal understanding only discernible by our innermost beings. We become a collective source of higher consciousness. Our common grief language helps us bond with those who resonate with our vibe.

So, Warriors, Let up, hoping other people share your pain with you. Embrace the idea that you are connected to a group of people who "get it," and you become a force that cannot be stopped together. Make use of your suffering as a starting point for introspection and growth.

In doing so, you give tribute to the unconditional love you shared with your departed loved one and become that twinkle who walks this path of grief.

In grief, we are chosen to carry
the unseen language of sorrow,
a testament to our love and
resilience.

Unveiling the Art of Respecting *Grief*

In this era of digital connectivity, we find ourselves conditioned to swiftly move on and brush aside the depths of our grief. Glossing over the importance of grieving and grief acceptance might be easy in today's fast-paced world. However, grief encompasses far more than prolonged sadness; it is an emotional journey that demands time, reverence, empathy, and patience to mend.

Loss, especially the irreparable loss of love, is at the heart of mourning. When we suffer a profound loss, it changes who we are and shines a light on what gives our lives true purpose. The path to recovery and growth lies in sincerely accepting our suffering.

Nobody enjoys being hurt, and most people will try to avoid it. However, suffering is a part of being human and must be faced head-on. Grief and loss, and the emotional sorrow they cause, are experiences all humans share at some point. Neither can we expect anybody else to take away our suffering, but we can show compassion, which can teach us a great deal about how to deal with the misery of others. Through compassion, we see that the suffering of others is natural and merits our whole attention.

The ability to empathize with others serves as a helpful reminder that there is no single "correct" way to deal with suffering. It is unnecessary to have all the solutions to be compassionate; all we need to do is be there for people when they are suffering.

So, when we see a loved one going through a tough time, let's not rush to ease their suffering. Instead, let's give our undivided attention to becoming wise. By doing so, we show them the kindness and consideration they deserve. There is an act of tremendous bravery, tenacity, and grit at the heart of mourning, an act that teaches profound truths about what it is to be human. So, let's not rush past the remembrances of limitless, unconditional LOVE.

Embracing the *Everlasting* Journey

BOTTOM *line*

One of life's greatest challenges is coming to terms with the fact that mourning is never really "done." We may reach a point where the raw pain of our loss has begun to fade, but the scars remain. These scars can be a source of strength and comfort. They remind us of the loved ones we have lost and help us appreciate life's fragility.

But keep in mind that you will never fully "get over" your loss. It is an ongoing journey that we all must travel. There may be days when the path is smooth and the going is rough. But eventually, we will reach our destination: a place where we can find peace and happiness again.

Healing is an ever-unfolding journey, an intricate dance of self-discovery and growth. As we set out on our journey, we recognize that our wounds are not who we are but a testament to our capacity to love fiercely and persevere through adversity. Unconditional self-love feeds the soul and opens the door to healing on all levels. Putting aside baggage and focusing on what brings us joy might help us find inner freedom.

You may find that your relationship with your loved one changes as you move through grief. Their presence becomes a source of strength and comfort, reminding you of their eternal love. You gradually rebuild your life as you heal, carrying their memory within you. Their spirit entwines with yours, illuminating the path to a meaningful existence.

While healing may never be complete, grief can propel you toward a more positive emotional journey. Embracing and expressing your grief healthily allows for soul healing to begin.

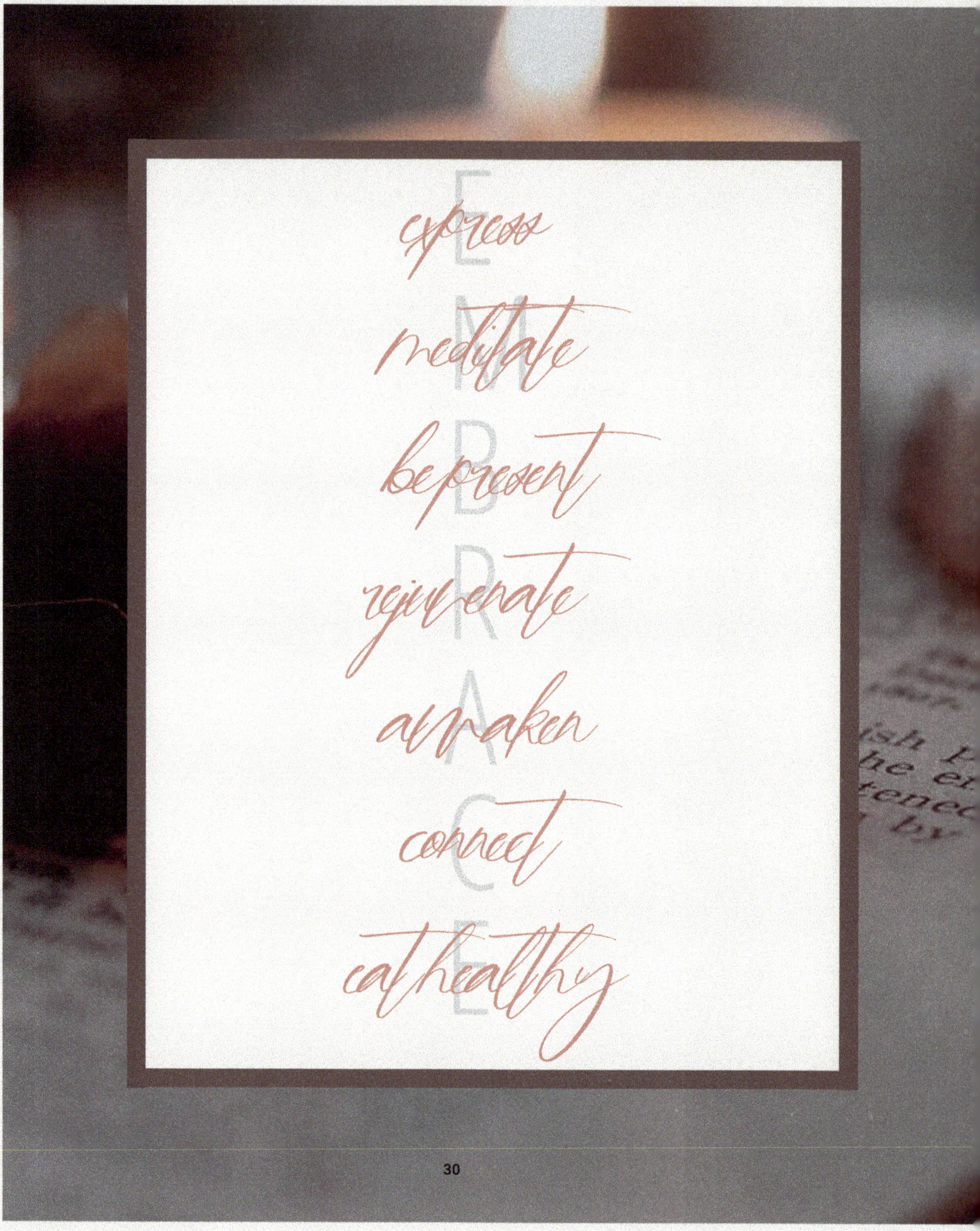

express

meditate

be present

rejuvenate

awaken

connect

eat healthy

E
M
B
R
A
C
E

DOES EMBRACE
Speak to You?

Explore the transformative power of The 7 Stages of GRIEF Alignment workbook journal, designed to support you authentically and effectively on your grief journey. Each stage of this journal is carefully crafted to nurture your physical and mental well-being, empowering you to strengthen critical aspects of your health as you navigate through the aftermath of a traumatic event. Embracing these stages will lead you to greater strength, resilience, and a revitalized sense of purpose.

Drawing from personal experiences of loss and trauma, I created the 7 Stages of GRIEF Alignment mini journal to assist those willing to EMBRACE in their healing process. Within its pages, you'll discover practices that have deeply impacted my grief journey, enabling me to navigate through the pain and embrace genuine growth mindfully. These practices have brought about timeless healing, from releasing old attachments to rebuilding a lost sense of unconditional love.

This eternal healing perfectly captures the beauty of "Healing."

Whether at the beginning of your grief journey or making progress, embracing the stages outlined in this journal can ease the burden and infuse joy into your life. Let's say you've had enough and are ready to start living again. Please join me on the 7 Stages of the GRIEF Alignment workbook journal's transformational journey, or go even further and earn your Certified Wellness Warrior designation.

Take a deep breath, stay resilient, and remember that even in the darkest moments, we possess the inner strength to move forward. Embrace this opportunity and witness its profound impact on your life. Not doing so would be a mistake.

EXPRESS

Welcome to the First Stage of Grief Alignment: Express. In this stage, we encourage you to unleash your thoughts, feelings, and trauma through emotional journaling. By embracing this practice, you voice your emotions and release anxiety, triggers, and pain.

Reflect on its meaning in your grief journey and explore its significance. Use your notebook as a place of refuge where you may explore who you are and how you got here. Allow your own words to heal and shape your spirit.

Three ways you can integrate 'Express' into your daily therapy:

Emotional Journaling
Write freely each day to express and process your emotions.

Artistic Expression
Engage in creative activities to communicate and release emotions.

Verbal Communication
Share your feelings with a trusted person or practitioner for support and validation.

Expression is the key to unlocking our connection, allowing us to co-create a reality rooted in love and acceptance. So say their name, share your story, feel every moment, and remember—you are here for a reason. And always remember—you are here with a purpose. You have the power to create. So keep expressing yourself—you have everything it takes to thrive!

How will you express today?

MEDITATE

Have you ever explored the richness of meditation? It offers a gateway to discovering tranquility and clarity in grief or challenging moments. By dedicating time to cultivating mindful awareness, we unlock the potential for remarkable revelations.
With each intentional inhalation and exhalation, we create a sacred space within ourselves, allowing us to confront our emotions from a higher perspective.

Discover peace in nature's embrace, where meditation unveils transformative insights.

Pause for a moment and ask yourself: When was the last time you truly paused and immersed yourself in the vivid reality of "here"? It is in the here and now, the ever-present moment, where true existence lives. It is within this moment that the miracle of life unfolds.

BE PRESENT

'Be Present' is the 3rd Stage of Grief Alignment, encouraging us to be still. Society often expects us to conform to specific standards, but we have the power to within ourselves begin a path toward wellness simply by showing up.

Being present allows us to reconnect with life, love, and feel again.

Let's focus on being present and mindful. Pay attention to your breath - feel the rise and fall of your chest and let it move like a symphony's crescendo. Focus on the present and feel the caress of each inhale and exhale. Take in the vibrant feelings that sweep your entire being, and let them merge with the present moment.

Allowing your emotions to take over can be liberating. Accepting and working with our feelings without hesitation or judgment is crucial. Whatever those emotions may be, it's okay to feel them. Take a moment to permit yourself to step back, allowing your soul to have time within this very breath.

REJUVENATE

For true revitalization, we must turn inward and examine our bodily, mental, and spiritual states.

It can help us reclaim our vitality and lead us toward joy and fulfillment, especially when dealing with the loss of a loved one or the constant stresses of modern life. Transformation comes with self-reflection, inner growth, and healing. You have the power to do this!

By embracing new challenges and striving to grow in every aspect of our lives, we can reignite the spark and fire up our souls. So, why wait? We can rejuvenate and awaken joy at every level with determination and self-acceptance.

Reflecting on our loved ones and the gifts they gave us can also help rejuvenate our lives in their honor. Whether remembering a favorite memory or reaching out to those who supported us during difficult times, each act deepens the connection between us and our loved ones, even as they move beyond the physical world.

Ultimately, we choose how to react to grief, but by acknowledging our journey and embracing joy, we can find strength in our spirit again.

AWAKEN

In the 5th Stage of Grief Alignment, Awaken, you are invited to embrace the essence of being fully alive and anchored in the present moment. Retaining and shielding ourselves from raw emotions and harsh realities is expected in the depths of grief.

Awakening is the key that unlocks the door to our inner resilience and rekindles our faith in the truth that lies before us.

Pause and contemplate your life as it stands today. Allow this fresh perspective to offer a broader view, enabling you to observe your journey from a distance. In this introspection, you may realize that all you need lives within, and a vast expanse of possibilities awaits you on the horizon.

Let's embrace the awakening, as it acts as a catalyst that propels us forward with a renewed sense of vitality and purpose on our journey.

CONNECT

In the 'C' of EMBRACE, we find the power of connection in the 6th Stage of Grief. As we make our way through the complexities of this world, now is the moment to strengthen our connection to ourselves, our spirit, and our mind. While it may pose challenges, remember that we all thrive on daily connections.

How will you choose to CONNECT today?

Your mind. Your body. Your spirit.

Make a conscious effort to connect with yourself by dedicating just five minutes to express gratitude, a walk in nature, engaging in reflective journaling, cooking, creating, or allowing yourself to be still. Focus on self-care and self-reflection to enhance your well-being.

Tune in to your needs and honor them, for it is in these connections that true healing and growth can flourish.

EAT HEALTHY

In the final stage of our grief alignment journey, we are called to embrace the importance of nourishing ourselves through healthy eating. As we have journeyed through the different stages of grief in our course, we have learned the significance of addressing our emotional, mental, and spiritual needs. Now, we focus on the physical aspect of our well-being, recognizing that what we put into our bodies directly impacts our healing process.

Eating healthy becomes the inner thread that weaves all the stages of our grief alignment journey. By nourishing ourselves with wholesome, nutrient-rich foods, we provide our bodies with the fuel to support our healing from the inside out. We actively participate in our healing process by prioritizing foods promoting strength, vitality, and well-being.

As we continue our journey beyond grief, let us carry healthy eating lessons. Let us embrace the power of wholesome foods to support our ongoing healing and growth.

It is through this holistic approach that we can truly thrive and create a life that is vibrant, nourished, and filled with joy.

YOUR INNER
spiritual warrior!

EMBRACE is the ultimate exhilarating journey of healing and transformation. This course is not just a certification—it is a profound commitment to healing and a powerful dedication to moving forward with purpose.

We encounter countless challenges that test our resilience and tempt us to give up. Yet, deep within us lies an untapped well of strength, waiting patiently to be discovered and unleashed. This course empowers you to tap into that inner strength, unlock your full potential, and become the vessel to *healing it forward*.

The key lies in listening to your heart and trusting your instincts. By tuning into the untapped wisdom at the core of your being, you gain the clarity and guidance needed to navigate any obstacle that comes your way. With a resilient focus, you cultivate the courage and determination required to **move with** emotional barriers.

As you EMBRACE this journey, you discover that nurturing your inner world positively impacts your external world, cultivating meaningful connections with others, and investing in your self-enlightenment. The key lies in listening to your heart and trusting your instincts.

The 7 Stages of Grief Alignment will be your guiding light as you EMBRACE each stage of grief in your own time. Recognize that these stages are not linear processes; you may move back and forth between them as you navigate your unique grief journey. This flexibility allows you to honor your experience and progress at your own pace.

Are you ready to step into your power as a Certified Grief Wellness Coach?
Sign up today and trust your inner calling, take that leap of faith, and let your guiding light illuminate the path of healing and transformation for yourself and others.

A Graceful Pivot to Purpose

Michele C. Bell's narrative is a profound testament to resilience, the transformative power of embracing life's most profound challenges, and the depth of human compassion. Her journey, which began with the deeply personal and original work "*A Journey of Unconditional Love*," evolved into the 22-time award-winning story, "*A Son's Gift*," marking the inception of her distinguished career as an empathetic voice within the realm of grief literature.

With a Ph.D. in Philosophy and Metaphysics, Michele brings a unique blend of intuitive insight and scholarly depth to "*The 7 Stages of Grief* - **EMBRACE**." This work, unlike traditional grief literature, opens a space where healing is interwoven with personal growth and transformation, guided by Michele's own experiences, her profound journey through PTSD, and her scholarly insights. This journey has not only deepened her understanding of grief and resilience but also infused her writing with authenticity and compassion, offering solace and a transformative roadmap to those navigating the intricacies of loss.

Her innovative approach, blending the profound depths of intuitive philosophy with avant-garde grief counseling modalities, pioneers a novel paradigm in grief literature. Michele's work, transcending meticulous writing and exploration, charts a path towards transformative healing. Each stage, encapsulated within the evocative acronym **EMBRACE**, is meticulously crafted to guide the bereaved with dignity, offering nuanced understanding through the labyrinth of loss.

Beyond her literary contributions, Michele's life story—marked by resilience amidst adversity—enriches her professional narrative. From facing challenges such as bullying and domestic abuse to navigating the complexities of being a holistic real estate broker, Michele's experiences underscore her innate desire to support individuals through significant life transitions. The profound loss of her son to Ewings Sarcoma tested her resolve, catalyzing a shift towards mental health advocacy and the development of groundbreaking methodologies like the Soul Design technique and the *7 Stages of Grief* workbooks.

Michele's contributions extend to her active involvement in suicide prevention and domestic abuse programs, where her voice has become a force for change. Her purpose, whether as a holistic real estate broker, end-of-life expert, or mental health advocate, remains consistent—to support, guide, and uplift. As a member and keynote speaker for the **Daughters of Penelope**, Michele shares inspiring messages of healing, humor, and love, emphasizing the necessity of such virtues in today's world.

At 58, Michele C. Bell, The Grief Warrior®, stands as a testament to the enduring power of the human spirit, commanding respect and fostering deep, authentic connections. Her life experiences, granting her the invaluable CAT credentials of **Compassion, Authenticity, and Trust**, continue to inspire those fortunate enough to encounter her legacy..

Testimonial

The "7 Stages of Grief" series transcends traditional grief support, offering a deeply compassionate and educational journey through the terrain of loss.

As someone who has dedicated over two decades to the pursuit of educational excellence and who has held the position of Governor for the New York State Daughters of Penelope, I've been privileged to witness the transformative power of community and philanthropy in education. Michele's work is a forward-thinking movement in this realm, embodying the essence of what it means to educate and heal.

Her approach to grief education is revolutionary, combining intuitive wisdom with a structured, empathetic methodology that guides individuals through each stage of grief in the **EMBRACE** series. The workbooks in educational curriculums would mark a significant step forward in our approach to emotional and psychological well-being, providing students and educators alike with the tools to face life's adversities with resilience and understanding the importance of emotional health as the foundation of a strong, resilient community.

I am confident that its incorporation into educational systems will not only enrich our curriculum but also fortify the hearts and minds of our students for generations to come.

Professor Lainie M. Damaskos-Christou
Governor of NYS Daughters of Penelope,
National Board-Certified World Language Teacher of Spanish and Greek

DISCLAIMER

All content within the 7 Stages of Grief Alignment Workbook is original and intended solely to promote mind, body, and spirit well-being. This material does not replace the expertise or advice of a licensed mental health professional. Grief experiences are unique to each individual, and while the workbook provides supportive tools and perspectives, it does not guarantee specific outcomes. If you are experiencing intense or extreme distress, please consult a professional.

By using this course, you acknowledge and accept these terms and conditions. The 7 Stages of Grief certification program, conceived and developed by Dr. Michele Bell, offers an innovative, holistic, and empathy-driven approach to understanding and navigating grief. It is rooted in comprehensive research and deep insight into the human experience of loss and recovery.

Program Overview:
- Embracing Growth in Grief: Recognize the transformative potential within grief.
- The 7 Stages of Grief: Explore the intricate emotional journey of grief, encompassing its multifaceted seven stages.
- Pivoting with Purpose: Equip yourself with practical tools to channel grief's raw energy into purposeful action.
- Understanding the Power of Resistance: Gain insights into the obstacles resistance can pose on the healing journey and learn strategies to address and overcome it.
- Coping Modalities: Discover and apply various coping methods tailored to individual grief journeys or to assist others on this path.
- Certification: As a culmination, the program offers a certification examination to ensure a comprehensive understanding of the 7 Stages of Grief methodology.

Engage with the 7 Stages of Grief, All-In-One Master Compilation program to acquire a compassionate and informed approach to navigating the intricate labyrinth of grief, whether for personal growth or as a professional commitment.

Remember, every voice matters in bringing light to the shadows of grief. By uniting, we can raise awareness and create a world where everyone feels understood and supported during their moments of profound loss. I deeply appreciate your commitment to this cause. Please take a moment to sign the **Loss Awareness Day** petition on **Change.org**, inspired by the heartfelt endeavors of Lisa Marie Presley. Together, we can make a difference.
With heartfelt gratitude and hope,
MiMi + The Grief Warrior ®

you've made it

You are now ready to **EMBRACE** our Sixth Stage:

— connect —

That's the blessing and power of **pivoting with purpose.**

What are the 7 Stages of Grief Alignment?
Express. **M**editate.
Be Present. **R**ejuvenate.
Awaken. **C**onnect. **E**at Healthy.

Healing begins with acceptance and alignment transforms us through embracing our circumstances.

**The empower of embracing is in your next chapter –
are you ready to turn the page?**

Table of Contents

WELCOME
let's reconnect

Grand Rising, Warriors!

Welcome to the Sixth Stage of Grief. CONNECT. We've explored the traditional five stages, but your journey is unique, and in between these pages, exercises and journaling will all come together. Making the journey less strenuous on our souls.

This workbook is created for you by someone who's walked this difficult path. I had no tribe when I faced my grief twenty years ago; let this be your guide to healing in a world that often falls silent.

I know you're still healing. Maybe you don't feel like you've even started healing yet. Wherever you are on your journey, you are welcome here.

Grief has the power to both connect and disconnect us from what we love. Even when surrounded by support and opportunity, we feel alone, like nobody understands. Like we'll never be the same.

Grief is a double-edged sword—connecting and isolating us. You're never as alone as you feel. Life will throw curveballs of chaos, but therein lies beauty.

Let's journey together, embracing the raw realities of now and what comes next.

Reconnect with life, those you love, and most truly, yourself.

**Thank you for embracing your true self.
You've earned this moment.**

Unveiling the Threads of Connection: Guided Mantra for Spiritual Insight

After completing every chapter, we will establish a sacred rite of interconnection. Embrace these instructions as a sacred scroll, guiding you toward harmony in the pursuit of aligning oneself with the intricate dance of body, mind, and spirit; it is wise to dedicate a mere twenty minutes to each exercise.

Repeat this mantra:

"In the tranquil embrace of my heart, I unearth the profound serenity within me. In embracing the present moment, I pay homage to the cherished memories of yesteryear. In embracing the present moment, I release the burdens of tomorrow's anxieties. By embracing the essence of the present moment, I possess the power to mold the very fabric of my existence."

Enlightenment is the profound odyssey of harmonizing with the depths of your inner wisdom, forging a sacred bond with the whispers of your inner compass, the reservoir of knowledge and benevolence that transcends the superficial veneer of existence. It grants you the profound ability to perceive the world in its unadulterated essence, unveiling the veils that shroud your genuine being. The journey toward enlightenment is adorned with contemplation, profound introspection, and ethereal encounters, where one embraces each passing moment and assimilates the teachings of life in unison.

The Art of Spiritual Connection
SPIRIT Walk

Introducing the 7 tools of contemplation, reflection, and mystical experience will deepen this meaningful connection to self.

In our quest for **CONNECTION**, we open our hearts to receive -- deepening our roots, nurturing our growth, and harmonizing our existence, honoring our truth.

On this sacred journey, we are exploring the concept of **HUMILITY**, letting go of idealism and attachment to embrace the essence of our most authentic selves.

Like a luminous aura, **ASPIRATION** beckons us to contemplate our inner realm and the splendor that envelops us.

The quest for **TRUST** becomes our most loyal ally, illuminating our path and guiding us toward the sacred equilibrium.

Inviting **TRUTH** into our landscape, its power enables us to open our awareness to the spiritual truth within our inner sanctuary.

In the pursuit of **GRATITUDE**, we immerse ourselves in the opulence of our human journey and nurture a profound sense of appreciation within our souls.

In this profound odyssey, we encounter the essence of **COMPASSION**, embracing the art of boundless tenderness towards both our souls and the souls of others.

"Every journey we embark upon is unique—some straightforward, others meandering, some filled with bravery, and others riddled with uncertainty. Yet, every journey, when pursued with honesty and sincerity, holds the potential to lead us to a destination where our profound joy aligns with the world's profound purpose."

Be still and relearn to love you.

LESSON 1

Let Go to Let Yourself Glow

OBJECTIVE:
To release what's no longer serving us
to make more room for what will.

A NOTE OF LOVE:
Give Yourself Space to Heal

We have both heard it too many times.

"It's time to move on. Get over it."

But you and I both know that's not how it works.

Moving on isn't embracing. Moving on is resisting what's in front of you. No — we must connect with our pain. Sit with it for a quiet moment. Make room for ourselves to heal so we can move WITH our grief.

But to make room for our healing, we must make space, starting with the other pains from our pasts that we have carried for far too long.

Whether in this life — or past lives — you've collected much cargo. Now, we're here to unpack this baggage and ask:
"Is this truly mine to carry?"

Your fears. Your limiting beliefs. Your bad habits.

Do these beliefs originate from you, or have they been inherited from your ancestors, friends, society, or the media? It's important to consider if someone else's unresolved trauma influences them.

Ask yourself what's not yours to carry — and release it. It's in letting go of what no longer serves us that we make more room for what does.

As you *move with*, you have more room to grow. You can move with your fear, pain, and memories. You already have for so long.

But some aren't yours to carry any longer. Allow yourself to pause - observe...

Be present. Look within. And allow yourself to release what is no longer — and never was — yours.

JOURNAL PROMPTS

Answer each prompt with at least 1-3 paragraphs. Give yourself time to reflect, connect, and sit with your answers.

Letting Go of Fear

What are some things that cause fear within me?

_____
_____
_____
_____

What is the origin of these fears?

_____
_____
_____
_____

Are these fears belong to me or were they inherited from someone else?

_____
_____
_____
_____

How can I rewrite this fear to serve my personal growth and progress?

_____
_____
_____
_____

JOURNAL PROMPTS

Letting Go of Limiting Beliefs

Reflect on the notion of "moving on" versus "embracing." How do these two concepts differ in your understanding of grief and healing? How might embracing your pain and sitting with it, rather than resisting it, impact your healing journey?

_____

_____

_____

_____

Take a moment to examine the baggage you've been carrying from your past. What fears, limiting beliefs, or bad habits do you recognize as potential burdens you may have inherited from others? How might releasing these burdens create more space for healing and growth?

_____

_____

_____

_____

Explore the idea of inherited trauma and its influence on your beliefs and emotions. Are there aspects of your pain that may not originate from your personal experiences but could be passed down from previous generations or societal influences? How might understanding this concept help you navigate your healing process more compassionately?

_____

_____

_____

_____

Consider the liberating power of releasing what is not truly yours to carry. What emotions or memories might you hold that no longer serve your growth and well-being? How can you create a safe and nurturing space to release these burdens and make room for a more authentic and expansive self?

_____

_____

_____

_____

EXERCISE

Let's start with your first Connectivity Practice. Take 20 minutes to connect with your mind, body, and spirit. Find your space—the root of a tree - sitting in nature.

- Start a timer and take a moment to appreciate the beauty in your surroundings. Whether you meditate, journal, or walk in nature, make a mental note of what you are grateful for and what you find beautiful.

- Embrace the tranquility and take on the task of pondering over things that evoke feelings of connection and inspiration.

Yesterday was heavy. Release them. The tale of tomorrow is yet unwritten. Let it be. Allow it to unfold. Today belongs to you. Embrace it moment by moment. Connect your presence, make today your own, and dwell in the present.

In the coming moments, seek your tranquility in the gentle rhythm of your breathing. Seek gratitude and the beauty around you. PAUSE. OBSERVE: Engaging in a period of meditation, jotting down personal reflections in a journal, or taking a leisurely walk in nature can all serve as valuable ways to reflect and gain clarity.

Caring for, loving, and healing what we feel estranged is difficult. We're here to rekindle this bond with yourself, so you can manage, love, and heal yourself again.

Be still and relearn to love you.

LESSON 2

Bridging the Gap Between You & Your Inner Child

OBJECTIVE:
To nurture your inner child, break free from your self-sabotaging patterns, and connect with your childlike joy.

A NOTE OF LOVE:
Reconnect. Reignite. Reparent.

Recall your youth. Imagine everything about your past self.

Do you think these instances feel like distant memories? Do they seem like faded, vintage photos or characters from a story of your past?

Your inner child always remains with you, but occasionally, we tend to move on without them.

Our inner child is the embodiment of naivety and fragility. Their presence is evident in our fears, choices, relationships, and sorrows. They sparkle through our inquisitiveness, inventiveness, and joy.

However, when our early years were shadowed with more suffering than joy, we often wished to leave them behind.

In doing so, the fragile feelings of desertion and solitude intensify.

Your inner child can undermine you. Not necessarily intentionally, but as a cry for acknowledgment. A plea for healing. A call for re-parenting.

Engaging in self-reparenting is essential to strengthen our connection with our inner child. There comes a time when we need to reconcile with ourselves and offer the stability, courage, and love we yearned for in those early years.

A NOTE OF LOVE:
Reconnect. Reignite. Reparent.

Reflect on the feelings you harbored as a young one—your inner child is still wrestling with these emotions.

What self-destructive behaviors do you find yourself caught up in? What recurring patterns trap you?

Often these patterns are all too familiar, but they remain fragments and remnants of our history.

As you navigate these emotions, you can extend your hand, connect and gain control of the steering wheel.

So, spend some time with little you.

Indulge in messiness. Let laughter, chirps, and playful moments envelop you.

Revisit your childhood favorite books, indulge in your most special shows, and let your curiosity and creativity run wild.

Embrace painting by numbers or coloring beyond boundaries. Peruse old pictures, and send grace to that innocent, mischievous smile.

Let your guard down, and let your inner child gleam without criticism.

Then, when you both feel secure in each other's company, you can clasp hands and progress together.

Offer yourself empathy. Break the cycle, and be present for them. Forge a bond with your inner child, and they'll unveil a new realm for you.

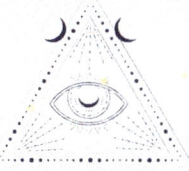

JOURNAL PROMPTS

*Step 1: Write a letter to your inner child. Give them the grace, compassion, and healing they deserve. Use these prompts to help guide your letter:

Write a Letter to Your Inner Child

What fears did I have during my childhood?

_____
_____
_____
_____

As a child, which emotions did I feel most often?

_____
_____
_____
_____

When I was a child, what were the things that made me happy, calm, and loved?

_____
_____
_____
_____

As a child, what were the words that I needed to hear?

_____
_____
_____
_____

JOURNAL PROMPTS

Reflection on the Past: Write about a specific memory from your childhood that stands out, whether joyful or painful. How does this memory impact your feelings and decisions today? Is it a memory your inner child holds onto tightly?

_____

_____

_____

_____

Letter to Your Younger Self: If you were to write a letter to yourself at age 10, what would you say? What advice or comfort would you offer? What praises would you share?

_____

_____

_____

_____

Feelings of Abandonment: Recall a time when you felt particularly abandoned or isolated in your younger years. How has that shaped your relationships and coping mechanisms today?

_____

_____

_____

_____

JOURNAL PROMPTS

*Step 2: Write a response letter from your inner child. Imagine what they have to say after receiving your first letter.

Give your present self the grace, compassion, and healing you gave your inner child. Use these prompts to help guide your response letter:

Write a Letter From Your Inner Child

Inner Child's Voice: Write a dialogue between your current self and your inner child. What are the fears, hopes, and dreams your inner child would voice out? How would you, as an adult, respond?

_____
_____
_____
_____

Visions of Childhood: Visualize a photograph from your past that captures a significant moment. Describe the photo in detail. What emotions are present? How does this frozen moment in time resonate with you now?

_____
_____
_____
_____

Steps to Re-parenting: List three specific ways you can self-reparenting to heal and reconnect with your inner child. How can you provide the stability, courage, and love you needed back then?

_____
_____
_____
_____

A Healing Moment: Think of a time when you acknowledged and cared for your inner child in a significant way. How did that make you feel? If you have not had such an experience, envision a situation where you could.

_____
_____
_____
_____

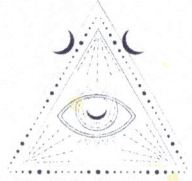

JOURNAL PROMPTS

What soothing phrases or affirmations can I offer to heal and reassure my inner child?

_____

_____

_____

_____

How can the insights from my younger self-guide and enrich my journey ahead?

_____

_____

_____

_____

How can I nurture and express love to the child within me and the person I am today?

_____

_____

_____

_____

INNER CHILD VISION BOARD EXERCISE

Purpose: To visually represent your connection with your inner child, understand past emotions, and visualize the healing and nurturing you want to provide.

Materials:

- A large piece of poster board or cardboard
- Old magazines, newspapers, photos, or printouts
- Scissors
- Glue or tape
- Markers, colored pencils, or paints

Steps:

1. **Preparation:** Clear a workspace and gather all your materials. Ensure you have a comfortable, calm environment to work in.
2. **Reflect:** Take a moment to remember your childhood and jot down any memories, emotions, or wants that come to mind.
3. **Search for Images:** Look for pictures that match your thoughts about your inner child in magazines or newspapers. They can represent memories, emotions, aspirations, or current desires.
4. **Cut and Sort:** As you find relevant images or words, cut them out. Group them loosely based on themes or feelings they evoke.
5. **Layout:** Before gluing anything, arrange your images on your board. Consider placing:
    - Memories or feelings on the left side.
    - Present feelings or acknowledgments in the center.
    - Future hopes, self-reparenting goals, and reconciliation on the right side.
6. **Embellish with Words or Drawings:** Use markers, colored pencils, or paints to add thoughts, dreams, or affirmations. For instance, you might write "It's okay to feel" or "I am here for you now" to emphasize the message of self-reparenting.
7. **Glue Everything Down:** Once you're satisfied with the layout, start gluing or taping down your images and words.
8. **Reflection:** Once your board is complete, take a step back. What feelings emerge as you look at the board? Consider writing a brief reflection or letter to your inner child based on the visuals you've chosen.
9. **Display:** Place your vision board somewhere you'll see it regularly. It's a visual reminder of your commitment to nurturing and reconciling with your inner child.
10. **Regular Check-ins:** Every few weeks or months, take a moment to sit with your vision board. Reflect on your progress in your self-reparenting journey and any new feelings or realizations that have emerged.

This vision board serves as a creative outlet and a tangible reminder of the importance of recognizing, understanding, and caring for your inner child.

LESSON 3

Find Wisdom in Every Day

OBJECTIVE:
Discover life's lessons by being mindful
of the wisdom and teachings
surrounding you.

A NOTE OF LOVE:
Uncovering Your Life Lessons

Life is our teacher. She's a challenging yet gentle one — she discerns when to reprimand when to reward, and when to let us navigate independently.

The problem is that we're not always the best students. We often stop heeding her lessons, assuming we know best, despite the stark truths before us.

However, once we acknowledge that we are simply learners in the grand classroom of life, we relieve the pressure of perfection. We can sometimes be 'right.' Everything around us doesn't need to be 'right' — our role is to learn from it.

If life speaks to us, our task is to pay attention. This perspective ignites our dormant childlike curiosity, bridging the gap to our inner child. We can explore freely if the world is our learning ground and playground.

Isn't it liberating to realize we don't hold the reins to everything?

Regardless of their scale, life imparts lessons daily. We must attune to them and allow them to steer us to our destined place, where we are meant to be.

Frequently, these lessons are unveiled in pain, sorrow, trauma, and tribulations. Even in monotony, stagnation, and solitude, we can unearth wisdom.

But we can only access this wisdom if we CONNECT.

We must connect to life as our teachers by EMBRACING the PRESENT and regarding our encounters and experiences as nuggets of wisdom, fostering growth, and illuminating truths.

A NOTE OF LOVE:
Uncovering Your Life Lessons

Become a wise observer and active participant in your life. Remember: You're the main character of your story, yet a background character for another. Find perspective in this. Seek to understand the stories around you, like a child enveloped in their new favorite book. Stop chasing what you need to learn and start embracing and accepting what's already around you.

Connect with yourself. Find the lessons already within you, waiting to rise to the surface. Get to know yourself in your actual, authentic state. Take time to get to know yourself and become aware of your life, mind, body, and soul.

This is where you connect with your life lessons. This is where you connect with your life's purpose.

Without learning, pain is simply pain. Without grace, grief is merely grief. We can thank human nature for our ability to create meaning, uncover stories, and build connections that turn pain into purpose and empower grace in our grief.

As a healing practitioner, I help my clients navigate the path to wisdom with a physical journey to an inspired destination. As we explore new territories, we map life lessons and pave the way to new destinations. This path to uncovering our purposes and unlocking our lessons often requires another guide.

Wherever you are, open yourself up to a new journey—a new destination. Leap and make a move. Show the universe and yourself that you're ready to receive wisdom. That you're prepared to learn, listen, and love.

Life is ready to connect you to your purpose. Will you receive it?

JOURNAL PROMPTS

Answer each prompt with at least 1-3 paragraphs. Give yourself time to reflect, connect, and sit with your answers.

Find Wisdom in Every Day

In what moments have I felt most connected to life's lessons, and how did those moments shape my perspective on growth and purpose?

_____
_____
_____
_____

Recall when pain, sorrow, or a challenging situation unveiled a profound lesson. How can I reframe similar experiences in the future to extract wisdom from them?

_____
_____
_____
_____

How can I deepen my connection with myself to understand better the stories and lessons that are waiting to emerge from within?

_____
_____
_____
_____

JOURNAL PROMPTS

Find Wisdom Today

When was the last time I fully embraced the present moment, seeking its hidden lessons and wisdom? How can I practice this mindfulness more frequently?

_____

_____

_____

_____

How does the concept of being both the main character in my story and a background character in someone else's impact my understanding of relationships and my role in the world?

_____

_____

_____

_____

Think about a time when life tried to teach you something but you resisted the lesson. In hindsight, what wisdom was life offering, and how can you open your heart to receive such teachings more gracefully in the future?

_____

_____

_____

_____

EXERCISE

Begin your next Connectivity Practice. Take 20 minutes to connect with your mind, body, and spirit.

- Set a timer and begin to look for the surrounding beauty. Note what you're grateful for and what you find beautiful as you meditate, journal, or walk in nature.

- You may approach this exercise with a curiosity to learn, the patience to pause and listen, or the willingness to receive wisdom.

LESSON 4

Reborn to Reconnect

OBJECTIVE:
To make peace with the present,
reconnect to this moment, and allow
yourself to Pause.

A NOTE OF LOVE:
The Power of The Pause

You're familiar with these age-old expressions:

"As one narrative concludes, another unfolds." "When one portal shuts, another opens."

We frequently perceive life as a ceaseless accumulation of objects, memories, and accomplishments. We devote days, months, or even years desiring and striving for our ambitions, only to immediately replace them with fresh ones. As soon as we cross off an item on our agenda, we hastily add a new one.

We run from life transitions. We fear being trapped in the "limbo," the waiting rooms of life — the periods where we're waiting to heal, for our opportunity, and for things to feel "normal" again.

But what if the healing, opportunity, and "normal" you're looking for are found in your life's waiting rooms? What if your reconnection lies BETWEEN your life's chapters and doorways?

This is what I like to call the power of The Pause.

The most profound way to heal is to engage with The Pause. You don't need to resolve all your issues or complete your list of tasks. There's no need for haste, no need to work tirelessly. Take your time thinking. Don't pass judgment. Pause.

Listen to your voice. Discover tranquility despite the upheaval. Allow yourself to adjust to this state of "limbo."

Ultimately, your happiness isn't contingent upon moving from Point A to Point B. We live most of our lives in these transitional zones. Thus, we reconnect with ourselves by uncovering serenity, strength, and meaning within these stages.

By allowing ourselves to Pause for long enough, we rediscover our purpose, vitality, and awareness.

Of course, this is more challenging in practice than in theory. Often, when we feel trapped in our life's waiting rooms, we've likely just emerged from our darkest chapters. We yearn to turn back time. We long to fast-forward.

A NOTE OF LOVE:
The Power of The Pause

We yearn to do anything but remain in this present moment of anticipation. Let's not deceive ourselves - it's a bitter pill to swallow. Our existence irrevocably alters when we suffer the loss of a person or an entity that holds significant meaning in our lives.

From this void arises the intersection of the "limbo" — unable to revert or leap ahead, things can seem gloomy.

We feel isolated. Perplexed. Disoriented. Truthfully, it's unsettling.

And it's precisely within these confines that we have two choices: to either sink further into the abyss or chart our course towards personal growth.

We shift our energy when we embrace the Pause and find a presence in this pain.

We realize that we've endured and blossomed through numerous transformations and transitions. We've lost so much and gained so much. We've greeted many new beginnings and bid farewell to various endings. We've adapted and progressed amidst daily changes.

And in these infinite shifts, we must seek The Pause. We need to move in harmony with our pain, not resist it.

Like sunflowers, we gradually ascend, grow, and turn toward the sunlight. Connecting to this moment, we pave the way for recovery. While it's slow and often invisible to the human eye, a gradual and ongoing process occurs.

Pause for yourself. Pause for the pain of others. Give yourself space to connect. This is our sanctuary for healing. This is where we reconnect. This is our place of rebirth.

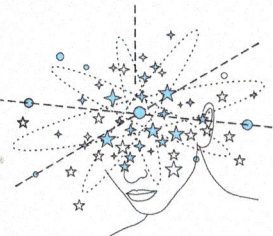

JOURNAL PROMPTS

Answer each prompt with at least 1-3 paragraphs. Give yourself time to reflect, connect, and sit with your answers.

The Power of The Pause

Reflect on a significant transition in your life. How did you initially react, and what did you discover during "The Pause" in that waiting room of life?

_____
_____
_____
_____

When you feel the urge to rush through a challenging moment, what are some strategies or reminders you can use to anchor yourself in the power of The Pause?

_____
_____
_____
_____

Think of a time when you resisted "limbo" or felt impatient with life's waiting room. How did that resistance serve or hinder your growth?

_____
_____
_____
_____

What rituals or practices can you cultivate to find solace and reconnect with your purpose during life's transitional zones?

_____
_____
_____
_____

EXERCISE

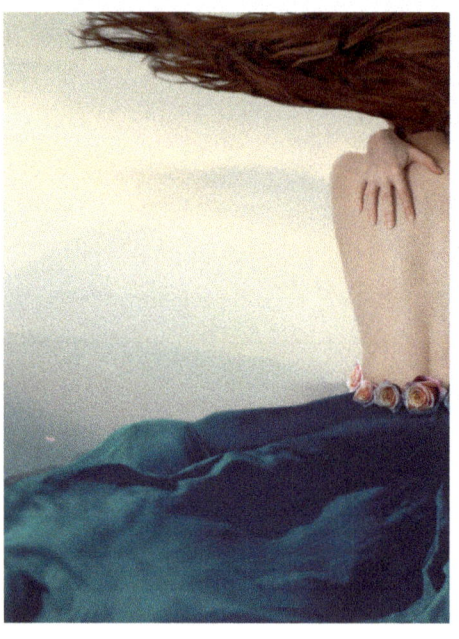

Start your next connectivity practice by taking 20 minutes to connect with your mind, body, and spirit.

- Set a timer and begin to look for the beauty around you. Note what you're grateful for and what you find beautiful as you meditate, journal, or walk in nature.

- In envisioning the impact you wish to have on the world, what meaningful endeavors or causes align with your purpose and can be pursued during this period of reflection?

- How can you ensure that your purpose during The Pause extends beyond this temporary break and becomes integral to your ongoing journey towards a more purposeful and fulfilling life?

- You may approach this exercise with a curiosity to learn, the patience to pause and listen, or the willingness to receive wisdom.

LESSON 5

Unbury Your Pain to Uncover Your Purpose

OBJECTIVE:
To explore our pains, heal our pasts,
and create a deep-rooted purpose.

A NOTE OF LOVE:
No More Pushing

We've been conditioned to suppress our feelings from childhood when distressing events occur.

Society categorized emotions as "positive" and "negative." We received praise for our laughter but were often discouraged when we displayed anger, sorrow, or vexation.

We were socialized to bury our suffering, to "maintain a cheerful exterior," and persist regardless. We're choosing not to take care of it right now... we'll manage it later.

We've become so proficient at concealing our distress that we occasionally lose sight of it until we suddenly can't.

Until one day, the pain resurfaces. We face a loss. Our past trauma revisits us. We endure the unfiltered pain of being human. We attempt to use the defenses of our younger selves, trying to bury, cover-up, and disguise our suffering. But as we suppress these emotions, they start to overwhelm us. As the saying goes, "It's the last straw that breaks the camel's back."

Burying our emotions only leaves them unresolved. They can fester, evolve, and warp how we experience the world. They can form blocks in our minds, bodies, and even spirits, creating physical manifestations of our trauma.

But in unburying them, we can begin to heal. We need to reconnect with our emotions, histories, and recollections to permit ourselves to evolve. Life is a cyclical journey. The past is not just "behind us." We don't simply "get over it."

Our existence is a continuous connection and progression from this precise instant. To fully engage with and EMBRACE the present, we must unpack our past and future.

When we hide from our pain, it doesn't disappear. It stays, feeling unhealed, unloved, and neglected. By burying our pain, we imply that our healing is unimportant when nothing could be more crucial.

But when we unbury, unpack, and unravel our pain, we can begin to understand our lives, ourselves, and our pasts. In this space, we can gain insight into our futures.

A NOTE OF LOVE:
No More Pushing

To feel pain is to find your reason for being. Every hero and legendary figure in mythology has a tragic history. They discovered what they were here to do after suffering loss, tragedy, or anguish.

Pain can guide us toward helping others through shared experiences. For me, it was the experience of grief and loss. As I grappled with an unthinkable loss, I sought out others in similar situations.

I thought, "We shouldn't have to navigate this alone." Today, I give others the same support, guidance, and resilience I wish I could give myself years ago.

How can you transmute your pain into a gentle, illuminated path for others to embrace?

What experiences are distinctively yours? What hardships have shaped, formed, and determined who you are today?

Embrace this. Engage with it. Allow yourself room to be present with your chaos. You don't need to hide it. You can be simultaneously battling and resilient. Disorganized and driven. You are grieving yet growing.

No more pushing. No more pushing away your emotions, your pain, or your past. We restrain ourselves through resistance but glow through acceptance, surrender, and embrace.

As you unbury your pain, you also unearth your purpose. It's time to connect with it.

JOURNAL PROMPTS

Answer each prompt with at least 1-3 paragraphs. Give yourself time to reflect, connect, and sit with your answers.

Unbury Your Pain to Uncover Your Purpose

Reflect on when you were encouraged to suppress a "negative" emotion. How did it shape your understanding of that emotion, and how do you approach it now?

_____

_____

_____

_____

Recall a painful or traumatic event from your past. How has this experience influenced your current outlook, behaviors, or relationships? How can you use this understanding to guide others or grow personally?

_____

_____

_____

What emotions or memories have you buried deep within, and what triggers or events bring them to the surface? How can you begin to address and embrace these feelings healthily?

_____

_____

_____

_____

JOURNAL PROMPTS

Answer each prompt with at least 1-3 paragraphs. Give yourself time to reflect, connect, and sit with your answers.

Unbury Your Pain to Uncover Your Purpose

Consider a time when your buried emotions manifested in unexpected ways – physically, mentally, or spiritually. How did you recognize the connection, and what steps did you take (or can take) to heal and integrate those feelings?

_____

_____

_____

_____

If your buried emotions could speak, what would they say? Envision a future where these emotions are channeled into purpose and passion. How can I view this impact from a place of purpose and grace?

_____

_____

_____

_____

EXERCISE

"Facing our pain uncovers our true purpose; it's not a burden, but a beacon leading us to our authentic path."

Begin your next Connectivity Practice. Take 20 minutes to connect with your mind, body, and spirit.

- Set a timer and begin to look for the surrounding beauty. Note what you're grateful for and what you find beautiful as you meditate, journal, or walk in nature.
- How do you see your experiences of pain influencing your unique path to discover your purpose?
- How might you turn uncovering your pain into a transformative journey toward realizing your purpose?
- Allow yourself to feel any emotions that come up. Don't resist any thoughts, feelings, or sensations. Accept, surrender, and embrace. Let it flow. You don't have to hide anymore.

LESSON 6

Follow Your Path

OBJECTIVE:
Trust in ourselves, make peace with the
present and strengthen our connection
with intuition and wisdom.

A NOTE OF LOVE:
You Have the Answers — Listen.

It can be scary when we allow ourselves to feel again. Overwhelming. Uncomfortable.

As we shed layers of security and accept the rawness of healing, we start to evolve and seek resolution. People may try to dictate the "proper" way to heal, grieve, or progress while you search for answers.

But only you know this answer.

You are connected to the Universe, your Higher Power, and your Source of Energy. When you tune into this connection, you replace fear with faith.

You find courage and confidence, even in uncertainty about the future! Remember – the insights you're seeking are already embedded within your inner sanctuary.

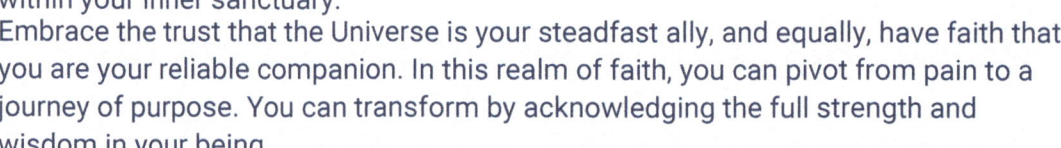

Embrace the trust that the Universe is your steadfast ally, and equally, have faith that you are your reliable companion. In this realm of faith, you can pivot from pain to a journey of purpose. You can transform by acknowledging the full strength and wisdom in your being.

When we contemplate "following our path," we often envision a grand, dramatic unveiling — a concealed purpose that will suddenly appear miraculously ready to metamorphose our lives one day.

But our purposes are already present within us. The answers you seek lie within your spirit. You have the inner compass. You carry an internal compass. You won't discover your healing trajectory by comparing it with others. Introspection will reveal it by taking a pause. Reflecting. Breathing. Your path will illuminate before you by simply existing in the present moment.

A NOTE OF LOVE:
You Have the Answers — Listen.

Ignite this bond with your inner self, and you'll unveil the wisdom within you.

Bear in mind: This is The Pause: each day, serene moments are utilized for reflection, connection, and achieving lucidity.

In these moments, we let go of the need to control, skip to the book's last page, and fast-forward to the end. That's not where the answers are. The answers you're looking for are in between the pages and paragraphs. They're in the very life chapter you're currently navigating.

Just because someone else is on a different chapter doesn't mean you're behind — you're merely experiencing other narratives.

Your decisions. Remember: You are the author. While you may not always be able to forecast every aspect of your narrative, you hold the reins to your destiny.

There's no universally "correct" way to mourn. There's no set schedule for healing. The journey manifests differently for each one of us.

Your journey through grief is uniquely yours. You will discover your path when it's the right moment for you. Trust the process, and have faith in yourself.

You have everything you need to heal.

Align with the power already present within you. Be patient.

Remember The Pause. The solutions aren't found in rushing forward but in breathing and existing here, in the present moment.

JOURNAL PROMPTS

Answer each prompt with at least 1-3 paragraphs. Give yourself time to reflect, connect, and sit with your answers.

Follow Your Path

The Pause Reflection: Consider a recent situation where you must rush to a conclusion. How might you have benefited from embracing "The Pause" instead?

_____

_____

_____

_____

Author of Your Narrative: What would the current chapter be titled if your life was a book? Describe the key events and emotions in this chapter.

_____

_____

_____

_____

In-Between Moments: Recollect a seemingly insignificant moment from the past week — something between the 'big events.' What wisdom or realization can you derive from this often-overlooked experience?

_____

_____

_____

_____

JOURNAL PROMPTS

Answer each prompt with at least 1-3 paragraphs. Give yourself time to reflect, connect, and sit with your answers.

Follow Your Path

Comparative Journey: Reflect on a time when you felt behind because others seemed ahead in their life's journey. How can you shift your perspective to understand that your unique narrative is neither behind nor ahead, but just right for you?

_____

_____

_____

_____

Healing Timeline: Write about a past wound or trauma. How has your healing process for this experience been unique? Are there any pressures you feel from external sources on how you should heal, and how can you let go of these to honor your journey?

_____

_____

_____

_____

Power Within: Identify a strength or quality within yourself that you often overlook. How can this internal power aid in your healing and personal growth? Remember to align with this power during moments of self-doubt.

_____

_____

_____

_____

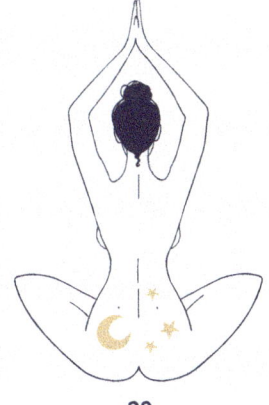

EXERCISE

Begin your next Connectivity Practice: Use the prompts blow to begin.

- Set a timer (30 mins each exercise) Note what you're grateful for and what you find beautiful as you meditate, journal, or walk in nature.

- Trust yourself as you reflect and connect. Let your thoughts and intuition lead, trusting that you'll be led to growth, hope, and healing.

Mind-Body-Spirit Vision Board

Craft a vision board that visually represents your path, not just in material or external achievements but feelings, growth, and spiritual aspirations.

Divide the board into three sections: Mind, Body, and Spirit. For the Mind, include images or words representing your intellectual growth, learning goals, or creativity. For the Body, display representations of health, wellness, vitality, or physical challenges you wish to undertake. Lastly, for the Spirit, choose images or phrases that reflect your inner values, spiritual growth, or a sense of purpose.

This creative exercise solidifies your path visually and serves as a daily reminder to stay aligned and connected with your mind, body, and spirit.

Journey Meditation

This exercise invites you on a meditative journey to connect with your path deeply.

Start by finding a comfortable, quiet place to sit or stand with a relaxed posture. Take a moment to breathe, allowing each breath to ground you in the present.
Now, gaze softly at these words and let them guide you. Imagine yourself at the beginning of a path. This path is a representation of your life journey. As you mentally tread this path, engage your senses. What might you see on this journey? Can you hear the subtle sounds around you? Feel the essence of this path and its significance in your heart. As you move along in your mind's eye, allow events or experiences from your journey to come forth. Don't judge or analyze them; acknowledge them.

Engaging with this exercise can offer profound insights about your current path, helping you align your mind, body, and spirit. As you finish, take a deep breath and let the feeling of connection linger in your journal. Whenever you're ready, continue with your day, carrying the insights and tranquility from this meditation.

Continue, Not Conclusion

Dear Courageous Warriors,

As the sun sets on our shared voyage in the CONNECT stage, it is a gentle transition, not an end. Much like a tale in a series of chronicles, our adventure prepares us for the next chapter.

As we journey through the 7 Stages of Grief, a powerful urge may arise within many of us, a longing to rewrite our stories swiftly.
Yet, I'd like to remind you of the ancient trees and persistent blooms. Their tale is told not in sudden leaps but in quiet, steadfast growth.

PAUSE. OBSERVE. DISCERN.

As we step into tomorrow, I invite you to join me in embracing our forthcoming chapter: Nourishing with Eating Healthy. In tending to the vessel that houses our spirit, we begin the alchemy of mending the soul. In cherishing ourselves, we praise our inner sanctum's worth.

For, in the end, what is truer than the act of self-love?

With Intention & Affection,

MiMi

Michele C. Bell's narrative is a profound testament to resilience, the transformative power of embracing life's most profound challenges, and the depth of human compassion. Her journey, which began with the deeply personal and original work "*A Journey of Unconditional Love*," evolved into the 22-time award-winning story, "*A Son's Gift*," marking the inception of her distinguished career as an empathetic voice within the realm of grief literature.

With a Ph.D. in Philosophy and Metaphysics, Michele brings a unique blend of intuitive insight and scholarly depth to "*The 7 Stages of Grief* - **EMBRACE**." This work, unlike traditional grief literature, opens a space where healing is interwoven with personal growth and transformation, guided by Michele's own experiences, her profound journey through PTSD, and her scholarly insights. This journey has not only deepened her understanding of grief and resilience but also infused her writing with authenticity and compassion, offering solace and a transformative roadmap to those navigating the intricacies of loss.

Her innovative approach, blending the profound depths of intuitive philosophy with avant-garde grief counseling modalities, pioneers a novel paradigm in grief literature. Michele's work, transcending meticulous writing and exploration, charts a path towards transformative healing. Each stage, encapsulated within the evocative acronym **EMBRACE**, is meticulously crafted to guide the bereaved with dignity, offering nuanced understanding through the labyrinth of loss.

Beyond her literary contributions, Michele's life story—marked by resilience amidst adversity—enriches her professional narrative. From facing challenges such as bullying and domestic abuse to navigating the complexities of being a holistic real estate broker, Michele's experiences underscore her innate desire to support individuals through significant life transitions. The profound loss of her son to Ewings Sarcoma tested her resolve, catalyzing a shift towards mental health advocacy and the development of groundbreaking methodologies like the Soul Design technique and the *7 Stages of Grief* workbooks.

Michele's contributions extend to her active involvement in suicide prevention and domestic abuse programs, where her voice has become a force for change. Her purpose, whether as a holistic real estate broker, end-of-life expert, or mental health advocate, remains consistent—to support, guide, and uplift. As a member and keynote speaker for the **Daughters of Penelope**, Michele shares inspiring messages of healing, humor, and love, emphasizing the necessity of such virtues in today's world.

At 58, Michele C. Bell, The Grief Warrior®, stands as a testament to the enduring power of the human spirit, commanding respect and fostering deep, authentic connections. Her life experiences, granting her the invaluable CAT credentials of **Compassion, Authenticity, and Trust**, continue to inspire those fortunate enough to encounter her legacy..

Testimonial

The "7 Stages of Grief" series transcends traditional grief support, offering a deeply compassionate and educational journey through the terrain of loss.

As someone who has dedicated over two decades to the pursuit of educational excellence and who has held the position of Governor for the New York State Daughters of Penelope, I've been privileged to witness the transformative power of community and philanthropy in education. Michele's work is a forward-thinking movement in this realm, embodying the essence of what it means to educate and heal.

Her approach to grief education is revolutionary, combining intuitive wisdom with a structured, empathetic methodology that guides individuals through each stage of grief in the **EMBRACE** series. The workbooks in educational curriculums would mark a significant step forward in our approach to emotional and psychological well-being, providing students and educators alike with the tools to face life's adversities with resilience and understanding the importance of emotional health as the foundation of a strong, resilient community.

I am confident that its incorporation into educational systems will not only enrich our curriculum but also fortify the hearts and minds of our students for generations to come.

Professor Lainie M. Damaskos-Christou
Governor of NYS Daughters of Penelope,
National Board-Certified World Language Teacher of Spanish and Greek

DISCLAIMER

All content within the 7 Stages of Grief Alignment Workbook is original and intended solely to promote mind, body, and spirit well-being. This material does not replace the expertise or advice of a licensed mental health professional. Grief experiences are unique to each individual, and while the workbook provides supportive tools and perspectives, it does not guarantee specific outcomes. If you are experiencing intense or extreme distress, please consult a professional.

By using this course, you acknowledge and accept these terms and conditions. The 7 Stages of Grief certification program, conceived and developed by Dr. Michele Bell, offers an innovative, holistic, and empathy-driven approach to understanding and navigating grief. It is rooted in comprehensive research and deep insight into the human experience of loss and recovery.

Program Overview:
- Embracing Growth in Grief: Recognize the transformative potential within grief.
- The 7 Stages of Grief: Explore the intricate emotional journey of grief, encompassing its multifaceted seven stages.
- Pivoting with Purpose: Equip yourself with practical tools to channel grief's raw energy into purposeful action.
- Understanding the Power of Resistance: Gain insights into the obstacles resistance can pose on the healing journey and learn strategies to address and overcome it.
- Coping Modalities: Discover and apply various coping methods tailored to individual grief journeys or to assist others on this path.
- Certification: As a culmination, the program offers a certification examination to ensure a comprehensive understanding of the 7 Stages of Grief methodology.

Engage with the 7 Stages of Grief, All-In-One Master Compilation program to acquire a compassionate and informed approach to navigating the intricate labyrinth of grief, whether for personal growth or as a professional commitment.

Remember, every voice matters in bringing light to the shadows of grief. By uniting, we can raise awareness and create a world where everyone feels understood and supported during their moments of profound loss. I deeply appreciate your commitment to this cause. Please take a moment to sign the **Loss Awareness Day** petition on **Change.org**, inspired by the heartfelt endeavors of Lisa Marie Presley. Together, we can make a difference.
With heartfelt gratitude and hope,
MiMi + The Grief Warrior ®

www.ingramcontent.com/pod-product-compliance
Lightning Source LLC
Chambersburg PA
CBHW041150120626
46547CB00020B/3166